Scrum Mastery

*The Essential Guide to Scrum and
Agile Project Management*

Scrum Mastery

PUBLISHED BY: Greg Caldwell
© Copyright 2019 - All rights reserved.

The content contained within this book may not be reproduced, duplicated or transmitted without direct written permission from the author or the publisher.

Under no circumstances will any blame or legal responsibility be held against the publisher, or author, for any damages, reparation, or monetary loss due to the information contained within this book. Either directly or indirectly.

Legal Notice:

This book is copyright protected. This book is only for personal use. You cannot amend, distribute, sell, use, quote or paraphrase any part, or the content within this book, without the consent of the author or publisher.

Disclaimer Notice:

Please note the information contained within this document is for educational and entertainment purposes only. All effort has been executed to present accurate, up to date, and reliable, complete information. No warranties of any kind are declared or implied. Readers acknowledge that the author is not engaging in the rendering of legal, financial, medical or professional advice. The content within this book has been derived from various sources. Please consult a licensed professional before attempting any techniques outlined in this book.

By reading this document, the reader agrees that under no circumstances is the author responsible for any losses, direct or indirect, which are incurred as a result of the use of information contained within this document, including, but not limited to, — errors, omissions, or inaccuracies

Greg Caldwell

Table of Contents

Introduction 4

Chapter 1 Problems With Traditional Methods 11

Chapter 2 But First, Agile Management 20

Chapter 3 Scrummage 33

Chapter 4 The Big Three 55

Chapter 5 Scrum Artifacts 75

Chapter 6 Scrum Events 87

Chapter 7 Scrum In Action 108

Conclusion 120

Thank You 128

Resources Page 129

Introduction

Scrum was created over two decades ago in 1995 as a more reliable and faster way to develop software in the tech industry. At that time, there was a clamor for an alternative to the Waterfall method, where software is created in stages following rigid rules. Project managers call the shots and make the big decisions. The autocratic leadership eliminates the opportunity to get valuable input from the people who are actually building the software.

Projects moved painfully slow because the team cannot move on to the next stage until the current stage is not completed. No one moved until every item in the checklist was ticked. As a result, delays in release became a normal occurrence. Instead of just being an anomaly, it became the norm.

With an inflexible method like the Waterfall, project management became a conundrum to project managers and organizations. How can a method with step-by-step plans and Gantt charts be so problematic? One would think that with all the tools and resources made available to the team, the projects would be completed on time and on budget. Unfortunately, most software development firms fail to deliver on time. Projects were notoriously over budget as well.

Why the sudden fall from grace for the Waterfall method? The sequential one-direction process had worked rather well on simple straightforward projects. But the business landscape has changed over the years. Software development and IT projects have evolved and became more complex. Customers demand more features that developers cannot deliver. It's not for the lack of talent or skill, but because there are massive impediments brought on by an archaic method. There was no flexibility and wiggle room for developers to work their magic.

Aside from the actual coding and programming, software developers were pretty much just waiting for instructions from project managers. If they are not coding and testing, they are waiting for other team members to finish their part of the work. It's not slacking or being lazy, it's just how things worked then.

Scrum was invented by Sutherland to address the faults and limitations of the Waterfall method. It was a radical change because Scrum was everything Waterfall was not. It was adaptive and has self-correcting mechanisms that address the issues of wrong product delivery.

Early adopters of the new method experienced a spike in productivity. Products or iterations of the products are being delivered on time and best of all, they were delivering something that brings value to the customers. It didn't take long for Silicon Valley to adopt the framework in managing their complex software and hardware projects.

Being part of a software development team in a time when IT companies are gradually transitioning to Scrum means knowing firsthand how difficult the process can be due to the sheer amount of unlearning required. With a drastically new way of doing, not everyone is convinced that it was the way to go. But when the benefits outweigh the inconveniences, people start to see the light. Scrum quickly became the standard in the IT project management sphere.

Although Scrum became the darling in the tech world, it was virtually unknown to other industries. Having worked as a consultant for a non-tech company, it became apparent to me that not many businesses outside of Silicon Valley knew that such a project management framework exists. This is quite ironic considering that Scrum's origins can be traced back to Toyota's production system, a non-IT company.

When Scrum was applied to processes in non-tech companies, they experienced the same improvements and successes that tech companies were talking about. It shows that Scrum can be applied to any industry and it will have the same positive results. It has transformed and is continuing to transform how companies plan and execute projects in virtually every industry imaginable.

But as they say, Scrum is easy to learn but hard to master. This is because some of those who try to master it still clings on to obsolete methods, creating hybrid methods that don't always work as anticipated.

Scrum can be overwhelming for someone who is used to the Waterfall method because the structure and principles are radically different. Mastering Scrum requires embracing the Agile principles that the Scrum framework is based on. Learning a new system means understanding the problems, flaws, and shortcomings of the old system. This is because if people turn a blind eye to the faults of the old system, old habits will remain. These old and inefficient work habits can creep into the new system, making it difficult to learn and master.

This book is written in a way that will help the reader understand why there is a need to switch to Scrum. It explains the problems of traditional methods so that it can help the reader better understand the new system. If they don't acknowledge the inefficiencies, inadequacies, and wastefulness of old methods, they will have a hard time learning and mastering Scrum.

Chapters are arranged in a way that shows the progression of Scrum. It introduces concepts as they relate to a specific process in the Scrum framework so that it's much easier to comprehend. Some real-world examples are discussed to show how companies are integrating Scrum in their work processes and reaping the benefits.

This book explains how projects are prioritized, how development teams are utilized, how mistakes and errors are rectified, and how projects are monitored and released. It also explains the Scrum mindset that needs to be developed in order to succeed in delivering high value to customers.

One would think that it would be easy to transition to Scrum if there's proof that it works better than traditional methods. There is a reason giant tech companies like Apple, Google, and IBM are using Scrum framework in their own processes—it just works.

Scrum Mastery

Organizations must buy in to Scrum fully or not at all. This book will help you to know the problems of faulty methods, acquire new concepts, learn real-world case studies, and apply Scrum concepts to your industry.

Greg Caldwell

Chapter 1 Problems with Traditional Methods

"There's a better way to do it–find it." –
Thomas Edison

Software development teams face a range of problems with varying levels of difficulty. To better understand the impact of the Scrum framework on software development projects, take the case of a hypothetical software engineering group tasked to create a fully functional hardware and software system. It's a complex project that required the services of multiple software and hardware engineers. The project team utilized the Waterfall Software Engineering Model.

Problem 1: Rigid Methods

The Waterfall method (and other Jurassic procedures for that matter), follows what's called a *phased approach*. The first phase is to analyze the requirements to understand what the client wanted to get done and delivered.

The team proceeded with the next phases where the requirements were implemented, tested, verified, and maintained in software production environments until the team reached the end of the software engineering lifecycle.

No matter how competent the team members are, their software project failed. It's not because of the lack of skills or resources, but because of the extremely rigid sequential chain of different phases that the team had to adhere to. They could not move on to the next phase until the phase before it is completed.

This poses a problem because if one phase is delayed, subsequent phases are delayed as well. This effectively overshoots the timeline. This is not only frustrating to the team, but it is extremely time-consuming and costly.

The project timeline is set from the start based on the requirements of the project. The project manager takes into account anticipated problems that the project could face. But the reality is that it's just not possible to anticipate all the possible setbacks while you're still in the earliest phase of the project.

Because there is strict adherence to the requirements, the team treats the requirements as complete and infallible. But that's not how projects work in the real world. The more realistic expectation is that requirements change throughout the project.

Why does it change? Keep in mind that the requirements were identified by the client and the development team's job is to implement them. It's possible that there is an inaccurate gathering of requirements. But more importantly, the requirements don't articulate the needs of the client.

About 60% of the initial requirements of complex projects tend to change over time for the simple reason that the changes were not foreseen during the requirement gathering.

The implementation of unnecessary requirements cost the team time, effort, and money, which could have been used for other undertakings that provide better value to the client.

The grave mistake is treating the different project phases as separate stages when they are working together in parallel with each other. Although the Waterfall method is not effective and efficient for complex projects, it can be used to implement straightforward projects with lower risks.

Before the Scrum framework was introduced, the team's work process is bureaucratic, inefficient, overly complex, and unproductive. But more than that, employee morale drops and people are less committed to the overall organizational mission. The whole organization suffers and it takes time to get employees to engage and commit for the next projects.

Problem 2: Organizational Demands of Leadership & Silo Mentality

Before Scrum, the focus is on meeting the demands of the organizational leadership. Teams must comply and deliver the product on a fixed deadline. There is strict monitoring of the progress of the project based on the phases.

Leaders penalize team members who go off-track, not because they are incompetent, but because there were unforeseen events that hindered the members from progressing to the next phase.

There is a huge expectation (and pressure) for the team members to fix the emerging problems before the scheduled delivery date. This brings out the larger problem of independent silos.

People who are tasked to work for the same project come from different teams and don't even know each other by their names. For instance, the software testing team is totally independent of the software engineering team. So, each team doesn't know what the other is doing.

What's the implication of these separate silos? It means that project managers borrow people and resources from these silos, making the arrangement temporary. So these temporary teams are dissolved when the project is completed and members move on to their next tasks and assignment.

There is little to no commitment on the part of these temporary teams because they were just chosen for their skills for one project. And because there's no mechanism in place for these silos to learn from their mistakes, they're bound to repeat the same errors. They are not compelled to commit to the business to improve the bottom line. They don't feel that they have a stake in the success of the company.

Problem 3: Change Management

With the Waterfall method, project managers and team members treat error handling as an exception rather than a natural part of the process. They view impediments, errors, and changes as unnatural things that should not have happened in the first place.

Unforeseen changes or errors in the software project lead to costly delays that affect everything. Because the delays impede the team from delivering the product at the set deadline, the project fails. Teams then look for someone to blame for the failure. This results in finger-pointing and unfair accusations. It creates chaotic working dynamics not conducive for projects to succeed.

Problem 4: Autocratic Decisions

Management styles vary depending on company leadership and culture. Mainstream leadership tends to operate the traditional way and have leaders who make autocratic decisions. This means that decisions are solely in the hands of the leader and don't take into consideration the combined intelligence of the teams.

Those who are doing the actual work have little say on the decision-making progress and they are often overruled over the course of the software engineering lifecycle. Decisions are shifted away from teams and work centers, and more towards managers who are not directly involved in the nitty-gritty of software development.

As a result, it becomes very difficult for the hardworking team to decide on matters that require immediate attention. Mission-critical decisions have to come from the top. Even if the leaders are highly competent, not being in the work center could lead to uninformed decisions and not well-thought-out judgments.

But the worst part of autocratic decisions is that employees feel that they are undervalued and ignored. It completely stops them from thinking of creative and innovative means to solve problems. Constantly being overruled also results in the collapse of employee morale, which in turn can lead to many other problems down the line.

Autocratic decisions discourage teams from sharing their inputs when they are needed the most. Teams tend to disengage because they expect to be shot down. As a result, the people whose contributions and decisions are needed are discouraged to engage.

These problems continue to persist because companies maintain a leadership that favors autocratic decision-making over democratic ones. However, many companies are changing the way they work and starting to adopt a more inclusive method where the team's combined intelligence, technical skills, and inputs carry more weight than the decision of a person who is indirectly involved in software development.

Key Takeaways

- The traditional Waterfall method of project management no longer works in the ever-changing business landscape.

- Traditional methods are rigid, autocratic, bureaucratic, inefficient, and unproductive.

The next chapter discusses Agile Management and the principles that became the foundation of the Scrum framework.

Chapter 2 But First, Agile Management

"Changing practices is one thing; changing minds is quite another" —***Mike Cohn***

Agile Manifesto

Scrum has fully embedded the Agile Manifesto values in its framework, that's why the terms Scrum and Agile Scrum mean the same thing. They both refer to the Scrum software engineering process.

The core principles and the underlying philosophy of Scrum is deeply rooted in the Agile Manifesto values which focus on the following:

- Individuals and team member interactions over tools and rigid processes
- Working software or product over comprehensive documentation

- Collaboration with customers and clients over contract negotiations
- Responding to changes over sticking to plans

These values are favored by Agile Scrum over traditional software development principles because they serve the stakeholders better and create value for them. They also elevate and enhance the software engineering profession as a whole, regardless of roles and career levels.

Self-Organization

In the traditional software development process, there is a project manager who calls the shot. The purpose is to organize and lead the team to complete a project. But in Scrum, there is no manager or team leader who tells members what to do. There is a strong focus on self-organization wherein members decide among themselves what tasks they have to implement and execute in order to deliver the goals of a Sprint.

It may sound like a chaotic way of doing things because there's no designated leader who ensures that everyone is working and doing their jobs. People coming from the traditional way of doing things may struggle just a little bit to adjust to a more consensus way of working.

Evidently, there is a learning phase for everyone. During this phase, team members will get accustomed to Scrum elements like Sprint Backlog, Daily Scrum meetings, and Sprint Burndown Chart. Once these things are integrated into their work process, they can get into the swing of things and will find that the Scrum framework makes much more sense from a software development standpoint.

Although there is no leader to speak of, each team has a qualified and certified Scrum Master to support the team every step of the way. Scrum Masters know Scrum like the back of their hands and they make sure that team members are on the same page.

It may seem like a tall task to expect everyone to agree to a decision, but if team members adhere to the core values of Scrum, they'll find that working together despite conflicting opinions is possible. Compliance and trust in the joint decision-making process are the hallmarks of self-organization.

Inspect and Adapt

Two concepts that separate Scrum from other software development and delivery frameworks are *inspect* and *adapt*. They are easy to comprehend but difficult to master and properly implement because there would be resistance and friction at first. Add the fact that team members are not yet used to the Scrum process.

To understand these two concepts better, it's necessary to look at how the traditional process works. With a project manager overseeing the project, there is the risk of not being able to foresee problems that can affect the project significantly. Worse, the team is not equipped to adapt to the changes because they are focused on rigid plans.

With the inspect-and-adapt mentality, team members follow a standard operating procedure to help them adjust their courses of action while they are running the project and not when the project has already been delivered.

Toyota's Improvement Kata was born out of the need to continuously improve the production process and move from the current situation to a new situation. It makes people work more efficiently and help achieve the desired results. This culture of continuous learning and improvement applies so well in manufacturing, but it works just as efficiently in software development and delivery.

Scrum's Inspect and Adapt has four steps that can lead to efficiency.

Step 1: Inspect. With their current technical know-how, resources, and capabilities, the team inspects that backlogs and determines how the project is coming along based on certain criteria and requirements. Inspect happens during review and retrospective meetings.

Step 2: Adapt. Based on the information from the Inspect stage, the team members, in consensus, determines the direction and forecast (vision) of the next steps of the project with a clear strategy on how to implement and execute the vision. Adapt happens during planning and backlog refinement meetings.

Step 3: Learn. There is always a lesson to learn from the process. The team keeps a log of the things that work and things that don't work. Being aware of these things allows the team members to improve their work or become more efficient in how they complete their specific tasks. Learning happens even during the work process.

Step 4: Restart. The team starts over from the first step and repeats as long as necessary within the given Sprint time frame (30 days or less).

Agile Principles

Agile does not stop at the core values; it expands on those values and defines twelve Agile principles that serve as a guide for software development teams. The Scrum framework adheres to these principles.

1. Deliver the product early or deliver smaller working sections of the product.

2. Ask for feedback from the client, customers, and stakeholders and make the necessary changes even if the project is at the home stretch. Customer satisfaction is the main goal.

3. Deliver working prototypes or versions of the product at regular intervals to the client or customers so that they know how the project is coming along and they can provide feedback and input to enhance the product.

4. Developers and people from the business side of the operations should work together over the course of the project.

5. The development team must be given all the support they need to ensure that they can get the job done as per the requirements.

6. Hold regular meetings where critical information and issues can be conveyed clearly, systematically, and effectively.

7. Measure the project's progress by the working prototypes or early versions of the product.

8. Developers and stakeholders of the project must maintain a constant pace throughout the project's lifecycle.

9. The team must start with a good design and use attention to detail to enhance the product and the process.

10. No matter how complex the product is, the process must be kept simple. Unnecessary steps or bureaucracy must be removed from the process.

11. Self-organizing teams work more efficiently. They are able to filter all the inputs and choose those that provide the best designs and architecture.

12. The team must reflect on what they have to do to become more effective. They

must be flexible and open to adjusting their behavior and process to achieve a common goal.

Even if the tools, techniques, and resources change, these Agile principles do not change. While the principles are straightforward, it does not mean that they are easy to implement. It still depends on the team how they would apply these principles to their current project.

It's normal for some team members to be resistant to these principles, especially if they have been doing things the traditional way. But then again, the people in the team must commit to the Scrum values, otherwise, the project would not go smoothly.

Adhering to the principles doesn't mean there will be no challenges and problems along the way. It just means that the team can make adjustments and rectify the errors without jeopardizing the entire project.

Platinum Principles

The Agile Manifesto and the twelve Agile Principles are the basis of the modern agile development methods, to which the Scrum framework is built upon. There are three additional principles added to augment the original principles to capture the contemporary agile thinking that evolved over the years. These are additional guiding principles to help teams transition to agile project management with Scrum as the framework.

- Eliminate formality.

Formality is not efficient and prolongs processes. It's better to be straight to the point when conveying your message to other members. For instance, there's no need to create a PowerPoint presentation when you can easily post a note on the board for everyone to see.

Compare the time it takes to create that presentation with the time it takes to write down a note on a sticky note pad and you'll see the inefficiency of formality. If messages are communicated directly, immediately, and informally, you more likely to get a quick response and you can get back to your work without any fanfare.

When formality is eliminated, the team will evolve and create a Scrum culture of no-nonsense approach to tackling a project.

- Think and act like a team.

If you ever watched a basketball game where a team plays like a team, you can tell early on that the team has a higher chance of winning than a team that focuses on isolation play.

In corporate America, people tend to be competitive with their peers. The cutthroat business culture is making employees act like everything is a competition. This is because they want to stand out, get the promotion, and advance their respective careers.

In Scrum, the success or failure of the project is heavily reliant on the team dynamics. By aligning the team to the Scrum values, it can create a culture of participation, engagement, and collective ownership.

This is why there is no Project Manager to captain the ship. The focus is on how the team can deliver high-quality products to make customers happy and satisfied.

When fancy titles are eliminated, it's telling everyone on the team that no one owns any area of development. No one is singled out for his or her contribution or skills; it's always looked at as a team effort.

- Visualize.

Writing things down isn't bad, but pictures, graphs, and diagrams work better when conveying complex instructions or messages. Scrum Team members are more likely to understand concepts better when these are presented visually.

Even in social media platforms, text with photos pique the interest of people and they tend to engage more. This is no different in the Scrum setup. Sending information visually is encouraged to supplement the text content. It doesn't have to be intricate graphs or charts; a simple hand-sketched diagram on a notepad would do. As long as the message is communicated in a way that is easy to understand, aesthetics is not a priority.

Key Takeaways

- The underlying philosophy and principles of Scrum are deeply rooted in the Agile Manifesto
- The twelve Agile principles serve as a guide for software development teams.
- Three additional guiding principles capture the contemporary agile thinking that can help organizations transition to Agile with Scrum as the framework.

The next chapter gets into the nitty-gritty of Scrum and explains the values and framework in detail.

Chapter 3 Scrummage

"Question whether there are any ways to improve how you're doing, what you're doing, any ways of doing it better and faster, and what might be keeping you from doing that."—Jeff Sutherland

Why Scrum?

Scrum got its name from the rugby term *"scrummage"* which is a method of restarting a play after a stoppage. In a game of rugby, players from opposing teams are packed close together like in a huddle to attempt to gain possession of the ball. It emphasizes the importance of working as a team to achieve a goal. In complex product development, teams are given challenging objectives and tasks that can only be achieved through teamwork.

Scrum came into existence to address the shortcomings of the traditional Waterfall method. Project managers stood by Waterfall's linear sequential process because it is quite straightforward and easy to manage. But as projects became larger and more complex, the cracks of the Waterfall method began to show. It soon became apparent that Waterfall was too rigid and project managers were having a tough time integrating changes that they didn't anticipate.

With the traditional way of doing things, project teams are able to complete the deliverables within 18 to 24 months, as expected. What then is the problem? The problem is that they were delivering the wrong products with the wrong features and capabilities, leaving clients unhappy and unsatisfied.

You might wonder why a project could fail spectacularly even when all requirements were met. You see, as teams go through the process of gathering all the requirements and delivering them within the deadline (say, in 24 months), the world around them had changed drastically that what could have worked in the first six months no longer worked after 24 months. The Waterfall method was too rigid that it didn't have room for constant and frequent inspection to see if the product is still relevant to the times.

So, in 1995, Ken Schwaber and Jeff Sutherland presented the Scrum framework and offered an alternative approach to handling complex projects. More than that, it addressed the inadequacy and limitations of the Waterfall method. By delivering small things in small increments and in short periods of time, it not only allows teams to develop the right products, but they are also able to sustain these complex products.

Scrum was born out of the need to take into account the constantly changing requirements. Instead of having a predictive process where you generate the same output following the pre-determined steps, you are doing frequent inspection and adaptation as the work proceeds. By factoring in real-world scenarios and accepting that unpredictability exists, you can have a much more accurate picture of the tasks at hand.

What happens is that the situation dictates the type of process to apply in order for the product to adapt to changes. It's all about getting products to the market and supporting it through its overall lifecycle.

Although Scrum is best used for software development, it can also be used for:

- Research
- Hardware
- Government
- Process development and marketing
- Managing organizational operations
- Marketing

Scrum Values

It's easy for Scrum teams to go into disarray when problems arise; more so if they don't follow a set of values to keep them upright. A firm grasp of the Scrum values is necessary for the team to succeed and thrive with the Scrum framework. If team members subscribe to these values, they can get things done and deliver a product that would satisfy not just the customers but all the other stakeholders.

For Scrum to work, everyone must work together and adhere to the following values:

Courage

Team members need to have the courage to deal with problems and issues that can come up at any time. They must feel empowered to take action to fix even the toughest problems.

There will come a point where the team would face seemingly insurmountable challenges. Team members may even feel unhappy with the Scrum ecosystem—at least initially—which may affect the overall dynamics of the team.

Teams will face tough situations wherein they will be forced to make hard decisions. But if team members buy in on the Scrum values, they will decide and act courageously in times of difficulty. It's the commitment to stay courageous that makes teams succeed no matter how difficult the tasks are.

Focus

It's important that team members are focused on the goals set out for them to ensure that everyone is on the same page. When team members lose focus, it could lead to friction and disagreement.

To ensure that everyone in the team has a laser focus on the project like their lives depended on it, they must be clear on two things:

- Identification of correct task or work

If team members are able to identify the necessary tasks to deliver the Sprint goal, then they are more committed to completing the project. The task and the skill set should match. If members know the things expected of them, they will work to the best of their abilities to deliver the best product that will satisfy the clients and stakeholders.

- Prioritization

Projects can be overly complex with different moving parts requiring different levels of prioritization. The team must then decide which tasks are more important. With prioritization, the team can operate like clockwork.

Fortunately, the Scrum framework has several built-in rituals and events to identify and prioritize user stories and tasks.

- ➢ ***Scrum Grooming.*** This is also known as Backlog Refinement Meeting. This meeting is solely focused on prioritizing the Product Backlog and nothing else. It prepares members before they go to their Sprint Planning Meeting.
- ➢ ***Sprint Planning Meeting.*** In this meeting, team members identify and realize the correct order of work and see the work

➢ **Sprint Review Meeting.** This is where feedback from stakeholders shows what things work and what don't work. It prompts the team where to re-channel their resources to have more successful Sprint reviews in the future until the next iteration of the product is released.

➢ **Sprint Retrospective Meeting.** In this meeting, team members identify certain aspects of their software engineering processes that need to be improved.

Commitment

Every Scrum team member must personally commit to achieving the goals of the team. Without commitment, members will lack in contribution and engagement. It's quite difficult for people to commit to something if they have no clear understanding of the bigger picture.

In the realm of Scrum, commitment is synonymous with obsession. To be successful in business and life, you should become obsessed with your goals. It's no different from software engineering goals. If team members don't have that kind of commitment, it would be easy for the team to stumble and fall even at the slightest impediment.

When teams "malfunction" from the lack of dedication and commitment, the team will start making excuses for the failure. The team will begin to create justifications to legitimize the failure.

In the Scrum framework, there must be no room for excuses. If team members are totally committed and dedicated to the project, it becomes a lot easier to solve problems and provide value to clients.

Respect

Every team member has different skill sets that can contribute to the team's success. Respecting each other's different skills and capabilities can

Scrum Mastery

go a long way in managing expectations and team performance.

Every member of the Scrum team should respect one another regardless of age, gender, race, experience, or level of competence. There is a tendency for people who are more experienced with Scrum to invalidate or dismiss the contribution of less experienced members. If there is respect, such a case would have been allowed to happen.

Openness

Part of being transparent is being open to all the work and challenges with performing and completing the project. Team members must be honest and direct when they interact with fellow members and stakeholders.

When these values are instilled in Scrum team members, you are taking the element of surprise out of the equation. With Scrum, there should never be a surprise because everyone knows what everyone else is doing. No one is trying to hide anything because there are regular inspection and adaptation. If anyone is trying to hide something in the execution of the process, Scrum will find it because there is transparency.

The kind of openness required in the Scrum framework is the willingness of every team member to be transparent. Errors and mistakes are less than optimal outcomes, but with transparency, they can be rectified at the earliest and could improve the overall productivity of the team and the quality of the work. Doing so would have a positive impact on the achievement of the goals and the overall mission of the Scrum team.

The Framework

It is important to remember that Scrum is **_not_** a methodology. A methodology tells you exactly how you're going to work and the exact steps you're going to follow. These steps don't often change because they are pre-determined.

Scrum is an empirical process that allows you to consistently and continuously inspect and adapt to changing situations. It enables you to improve and enhance your process team by team and group by group.

You'll find a lot of difficulties if you try to assemble a team and force them to work in a certain way. This is because teams work differently. What you need to establish is transparency wherein one team knows what the other teams are doing, making sure that teams are constantly inspecting and adapting.

What Scrum does is implement the empirical process.

- **Transparency** – Everyone in the team knows what's going on
- **Adaptation** – Teams change tactical direction depending on the situation
- **Inspection** – Look at what teams do and how they do it

There is a dynamic process where teams are allowed to change based on the learning and based on the new knowledge brought on by different situations. The process evolves through constant inspection.

To simplify, the entire process revolves around these three things:
1. What the team is doing
2. How teams are doing it
3. What teams need to change to get to where they want to be

The Scrum framework is not as complex as it looks. Everything looks complicated when you're still starting with a new process, but Scrum is really a simple framework that's easy to understand and implement, however, mastering it is difficult because the team is constantly inspecting and adapting.

But before you master Scrum, you have to start at the very beginning and that's to understand the elements of the Scrum framework—from sprint planning to delivery.

Scrum Mastery

The Scrum framework lets team members know what their responsibilities are. It allows them to inspect and evaluate every element in the cycle and introduce new elements when they receive feedback. It's a very dynamic framework to ensure that the product is relevant and the right one for the stakeholders.

Scrum operates in a 3-3-5 framework:

- Three Artifacts
    - ✓ Product Backlog
    - ✓ Sprint Backlog
    - ✓ Product Increment

- Three Roles
    - ✓ Product Owner
    - ✓ Scrum Master
    - ✓ Development Team

- Five Events

- ✓ Product Backlog Refinement
- ✓ Sprint Planning
- ✓ Daily Scrum
- ✓ Sprint Review
- ✓ Sprint Retrospective

The Scrum Team and Governance

Product Owner

The job of the product owner is to maximize the value of the product and manage the product backlog. It's also part of the job to work with different stakeholders, whether internal or external.

The product owner is ultimately responsible and accountable for the product. There is only one product owner, but it doesn't mean he or she works alone. In fact, the product owner engages with different stakeholders to get important pieces of information to help deliver value back out to stakeholders and end users.

The primary responsibilities of the product owner are to:

- Maximize the value of the product
- Manage the product backlog
- Decide on what product and when to release it
- Act as a representative of stakeholders and customers to the Development Team

Scrum Master

The job of the Scrum Master is to ensure that the team understands what they are doing and that they are working well together. He or she is the person who removes any impediments that the team may encounter.

Team members need guidance and support when it comes to understanding the Scrum framework, values, practices, and rules. The Scrum Master must be able to help members make sense of the Scrum guide so that they adhere to the framework.

Contrary to popular belief, the Scrum Master is not the Project Manager. He or she guides the Scrum team members as they're working to self-organize. They cut impediments and ensure that everything that the team needs is there to deliver the products.

The primary responsibilities of the Scrum Master are to:

- Help team members understand the Scrum framework as defined in the Scrum Guide
- Provide support and ensure that the resources needed by the team are available
- Cut impediments to create a working environment where the Development Team can deliver and succeed

Development Team

The job of the Development Team is to get things done and deliver the right product.

Members of the team have specific expertise and specialization to self-organize and work in a series of sprints.

Team members create and develop the product and ensure that they meet the goals of the project based on the requirements and make the necessary adjustments. They engage and collaborate with the Product Owner to ensure that they are doing things right.

The primary responsibilities of the Development Team are to:

- Create the product and the product increment
- Self-organize itself and its work process
- Work and operate in a series of Sprints to get the job done
- Collaborate with the Product Owner to ensure that the team is working towards maximizing value

Stakeholders

Stakeholders are internal or external entities that have a stake in the project and are impacted by the actions of the Scrum Team through the product or increments they deliver.

- Internal stakeholders are from within the company that could be from any department, division, or branch. They could be from sales, marketing, human resources, or legal.
- External stakeholders could be the end-users, customers, or investors.

Benefits of Scrum

If done correctly, the Scrum framework can have the following positive effects to the team and the company:

- Better product quality that meets or exceeds client expectations

- More frequent code deployments (which means visitors to a site or users of the software or app can use the product and benefit from it through bug fixes, added features, or upgrades)
- Faster lead time from committing to the project all the way through to code deployment
- Lower change failure rate
- Reduced costs of deployments
- Improved employee motivation
- Improved organizational performance as a result of faster delivery of better or superior product
- Improved overall productivity
- Improved market penetration, increased market share, and higher profitability

Companies that utilize the Scrum framework find themselves able to adapt to the ever-changing requirements of clients and stakeholders with less chaos and confusion.

They know that they're creating a product that will remain relevant even if there are sudden changes in requirements. It's a win-win situation for the Scrum Team and the stakeholders.

Key Takeaways

- As projects became larger and more complex, the flaws of traditional methods of managing projects are exposed.
- Ken Schwaber and Jeff Sutherland presented the Scrum framework as an alternative approach to handling complex projects.
- Scrum will only work if teams work together and adhere to the Scrum values of Courage, Focus, Commitment, Respect, and Openness.
- Scrum implements the empirical process of transparency, adaptation, and inspection.

- Scrum operates in a 3-3-5 framework where there are 3 Artifacts, 3 Roles, and 5 Events.
- If the Scrum framework is implemented correctly, the organization stands to gain tremendous benefits that can have a positive effect on productivity and profitability.

The next chapter discusses the three important roles that make up the Scrum Team and details their responsibilities and functions.

Chapter 4 The Big Three

"If you focus on the strength of the team, you will begin to find work as a positive challenge."
— ***Salil Jha***

The Product Owner

The Product Owner does not own the product in the literal sense, but he or she represents the clients, customers, and other stakeholders. Only one person is designated as the Product Owner, not a group of people calling the shots. The focus is on delivering the right product to the customers. Maximizing value is always a priority to meet or exceed project requirements.

Not to be confused with a Project Manager, the Product Owner takes care of the business side of things—return on investment, prioritization, requirements. But more than that, the Project Owner ensures that technical and business priorities are aligned with each other. This is critical because it ensures that the product being developed is what the client needs.

Main Responsibilities of the Product Owner

- Identifies the goals and vision for the product
- Writes the vision statement
- Creates and maintains the Scrum Team Roadmap which contains the scope of the product and the relevant product backlog
- Takes ownership and responsibility of the product backlog
- Makes critical decisions concerning prioritizations and trade-offs
- Accepts and compiles feedback and adds them to the product backlog by level of priority
- Sets Sprint Goals and Release Goals
- Determines the product backlog that will go into the next Sprint
- Ensure that all product backlogs are visible to all Scrum team members

- Takes care the business side of the project and balances the business risk and the return on investment

- Makes himself/herself available to the development team throughout the working day to ensure that the team has a direct line of communication

- Accepts or rejects work results throughout the daily Sprint

- Decides which product increments are releasable or not

- Manages the expectations of customers and stakeholders

Evidently, the Product Owner plays a central role within the Scrum framework. The role not only unifies the product with the project management tasks and activities, but it also seamlessly integrates development and delivery.

Everything that the Scrum Team does is closely monitored by the Product Owner so that he or

Scrum Mastery

she can effectively coordinate their activities over the course of the project's lifecycle.

Given the enormous responsibility, the Product Owner can delegate some activities but the accountability remains with him or her.

Managing the Product Backlog

The Product Owner is the only person permitted to own the contents of the product backlog—from creation to maintenance to prioritization. He or she ensures that all members of the Scrum team comprehend the user stories in the product backlog and implements them accordingly.

To manage the product backlog, the Product Owner has to:

- Create and maintain the user stories in the product backlog

- Describe and explain the user stories in a clear and precise manner

- Prioritize user stories and align them with the business goals so that the team can fulfill the requirements of the product

- Ensure that everyone in the team understands the user stories in the product backlog so that they can implement them over the course of the Sprint

The Product Owner is not someone who tells everybody what they ought to do. What he or she can do is to clarify the objective and prioritize requirements. Part of the job is to minimize distractions so as to set an environment that is conducive for the development team to thrive and work efficiently with little to no supervision.

Since the Product Owner decides which requirements to pursue, he or she can also guide the team when they can shift from those requirements and move on to the next.

What the Product Owner can't do is tell the development team how much of the project they can do because there are different variables affecting that part of the task that only the development team can handle better than anyone else. All the Product Owner can do is to let them know what project they should work on based on priority.

A Product Owner is the main point of contact of team members whenever they need clarifications on the objectives and requirements. The Product Owner does not impose on team members how the work should be done, he or she only ensures that the work is done.

With the help of the Scrum Master, the Product Owner aims to create an environment where distractions to the team are minimized. Together, they deflect any business noise that could affect the development team. They are there to ensure that the development team does not have to deal with any business-related distractions.

It's important to note here that any member of the development team can contact and communicate with the stakeholders or other individuals outside of the team if they need clarifications on something they are working on. Keep in mind that Scrum eliminates bureaucracy so this kind of interaction is allowed.

Managing the Release of Product

Every project team aims to deliver a quality product that provides value to customers. A Product Owner ensures that the team accomplishes the project goals. To do so, he or she has to create and maintain a release plan. The release plan helps the Product Owner decide on product deliveries, end-user functionalities, and the order they need to be delivered.

To have all the needed data and information for the release plan, the Product Owner has to collaborate with the team members on a regular basis. This is a way to further enhance, fine-tune, and prioritize, as well as estimate user stories.

Aside from the development aspect of the project, the Product Owner also manages budgets and costs. So, it's really a challenging role that requires balancing the business aspect and the development side of the project.

Why Product Owners Prefer Scrum Framework Over Rigid Management Methods

- They are able to align the functions of the business and the development teams.

- They are able to forecast cost more accurately because there is daily progress.

- They know that at the end of every Sprint, there is a fully functioning and shippable product ready to go.

- They can get customer feedback continuously from the beginning to the end.

- They are able to know the return on investment at the end of every Sprint because there is a functional product being delivered.

- They know that with the flexible setup of the Scrum framework, the entire Scrum team can adapt to the ever-changing business needs and incorporate new requirements or rectify errors as soon as they are discovered.

The Scrum Master

If you think the role of the Scrum Master is as intimidating as it sounds, perhaps you have every reason to think that way. The role of the Scrum Master is to ensure that everyone in the team adheres to the Scrum framework. He or she coaches the team to develop norms and standards that comply with Scrum.

The primary responsibilities of the Scrum Master are to:

- Ensure that the Scrum framework is implemented in the business and development team ecosystem

- Coach the Scrum team as they adjust to processes and act towards the fulfillment of the project

- Make sure that the team members understand the Scrum values and commit to these values

- Ensure that the Scrum Product Owner and the Scrum Team are working together as efficiently as possible with each other

- Eliminate impediments to the continuity of work

- Shield the Scrum from outside interruptions and external interference so that the team is not distracted and could work in peace

You may have noticed that there may be an overlap in the responsibilities between the Project Owner and the Scrum Master but only in terms of eliminating interruptions, distractions, and interferences. In that aspect, they perform a similar role. But to understand the delineation of roles, think of it this way—the Product Owner directs the team while the

Scrum Master enables the team to work towards a common goal. In that sense, you'll be able to tell one from the other.

The Scrum Master is well-versed in the Scrum framework and is considered an expert in all things Scrum. But it doesn't mean that's the only thing he's good at. He or she must also possess people skills. Diplomacy and exceptional communication skills are necessary to talk to a diverse group of people who make up the Scrum team. In return, the team must respect the Scrum Master and trust that he or she can help the team resolve difficult problems.

Ideally, the Scrum Master should be chosen by the team, but in practice, the management decides who the Scrum Master should be. It's important that the Scrum Master works with one team full-time. Although it's possible that a Scrum Master can work on multiple teams, it is not recommended because the focus would be split between teams, which could result in issues down the line.

What the Scrum Master is not

There are many misconceptions and false notions about what the Scrum Master actually does. Perhaps the term "Master" makes people assume that the role is that of an infallible guru that has all the answers to all software development problems. Of course, no such superhuman exists.

To better understand the role of a Scrum Master, it's necessary to dispel the myths about Scrum Masters.

- ***The Scrum Master is not above the team.*** Many people tend to think that a Scrum Master's role is similar to a Project Manager who lords over the team. This can't be further from the truth. Keep in mind that there is no "boss" in the Scrum Team, but there is one person held accountable for the project or product and that's the Product Owner. In a self-managed team, there is no one person who has a higher position or rank. So in that sense, the Scrum Master is not above the team.

- ***The Scrum Master's suggestions and ideas are not always accepted.*** Being the expert in Scrum does not make the person's suggestions Gospel truths. The team will take them into consideration but ultimately, the team will implement the idea that is best for the project even if it doesn't come from the Scrum Master.

- ***The Scrum Master is less important than the Product Owner.*** For some reason, people are comparing and gauging each role's importance to determine which one is better or carries more weight. To set the record straight, both roles are extremely important to the success of the team. They have completely different functions that comparing them is pointless.

Self-managed teams that thrive under the Scrum framework have a high level of maturity, are committed to the goals, have respect for one another, and work with a proactive mindset, which somehow appears to dilute the responsibilities of the Scrum Master. But keep in mind that not all teams will start out as efficient as a well-oiled machine, hence the need for a Scrum Master.

The Scrum Master helps the team members understand the common objectives so that they can create a solid plan to achieve them. As a facilitator, the Scrum Master:

- Remains neutral and don't favor one side over the other
- Encourages members to do their best thinking and practices
- Promotes collaboration, engagement, and synergy
- Provides charismatic authority

Some developers see Scrum Masters as guardians because they protect the team from superficial events or activities that are not necessary. They minimize the business noise that distracts and derails the flow of work.

The Development Team

The development team is comprised of individuals who are capable of creating a shippable increment to the product. They can be software engineers, programmers, testers, marketers, analysts, and other key personnel depending on what the product is. Whatever the case, the development team is supported by the Product Owner and the Scrum Master.

Members of the development team implement the requirements of the software and they make a joint decision on how to deliver the best possible product increment during the Sprint.

These bunch of high-performers, as a solid team, have the following characteristics:

- Autonomous
- Self-organized
- Small
- Full-time
- Cross-functional

- Work in the same room (not in separate silos)

The team dynamics in Scrum moves away from the traditional practice of waiting for tasks to be given to members of the team. Instead, the team volunteers to own the tasks. The members are empowered to work for a common goal. There's a sense of pride and team spirit in taking on a project that they consider their own.

Again, keep in mind that a Scrum Team does not start as a well-oiled machine. In the beginning, it may be chaotic and without a clear direction. After all, they are an assembly of individuals with different skills and expertise.

With the help of the Scrum Master, a more cohesive team is developed. The more they learn about what Scrum is all about, they start to embody the principles of transparency, inspection, and adaptability. They develop the ability to utilize efficient processes, communicate better with one another, and take ownership of the project.

Size and Proximity

The Development Team can have a maximum of ten dedicated and full-time members. It is just the right size to enable the team to become independent and self-organized. Bigger teams can lead to more elaborate and complicated processes that can be inefficient and costly.

Collaboration is a key factor in a cross-functional team. With a small team, members can bring up an idea from start to finish in less time. This is because the inputs and discussions can be much more focused.

Proximity in Scrum is also an important consideration when choosing members of the Development Team. Keep in mind that this cross-functional team consists of people with complementary skills. If they work from different locations, communication is most likely done through email or chat. What's the problem with this kind of setup? It causes delays and adds more unnecessary processes, which defeats the purpose of Agile Scrum.

The solution is to put everyone in one big room where they could work closely together, literally. This kind of setup encourages open communication and quick response. Working in the same room eliminates writing an email for things that can be done verbally. The waiting time for a response is drastically reduced.

Being in the same room is also conducive for spontaneous exchange of ideas. Sometimes, spur-of-the-moment ideas can help with finding solutions to problems. There's no need to call meetings frequently when members are in close proximity to one another.

The benefits of a small-sized co-located team are:

- Face-to-face communication allow members to better understand the messages conveyed because they can hear the tone of voice, see the facial expressions, and understand concepts when illustrated on whiteboards and sticky notes.

- Team members can receive an immediate response with their inquiries.

- Everyone knows and understands what everyone is working on.

- There are fewer errors, defects, or wasted effort because there are fewer misunderstandings in the workflow or process.

- There are cost savings when unnecessary processes are eliminated.

There may be extraordinary circumstances that may require the company to outsource the work. In this case, it is suggested that a local product owner is hired for the job to work directly with the outsourced co-located Scrum Team.

Key Takeaways

- The three main roles that make up the Scrum Team are: the Product Owner, the Scrum Master, and the Development Team.

- Different sets of responsibilities for the roles create unique team dynamics conducive for success.

The next chapter introduces the Scrum Artifacts and explains the elements that make Scrum unique in the execution and implementation of a project.

Greg Caldwell

Chapter 5 Scrum Artifacts

"Greatness can't be imposed; it has to come from within. But it does live within all of us" –
Jeff Sutherland

Scrum Artifacts are elements that provide key information that the team and stakeholders need to be aware of in order to understand the product under development, the activities that need to be done, and the processes involved in the project.

1. Product Backlog

The Product Backlog is an ordered list of requirements needed in the product. It serves as a collection point for feedback received from the customer, stakeholders, and the Development Team. It is in a constant state of flux. So, new items are added to the list as they become available. It's managed by the Product Owner.

Here are some examples of valid Product Backlog Items (PBIs):

- Feature Definitions
- Constraints
- Behaviors
- User Actions or User Stories
- Bugs and Defects
- Use Cases
- Desirements
- Non-Functional Requirements

The team is not limited to working with these product backlogs nor are they restrained by specific items. There's nowhere in the Scrum Guide that says this is how the team will define the backlog items. It also does not indicate which ones to use. The rule of thumb is to use what's right for the team based on clear acceptance criteria.

As Scrum is all about inspecting and adapting, the team is free to use the backlog items that they are more comfortable with. They can use cases or a combination of PBIs. Ultimately, it will depend on how the team defines its process within Scrum.

Despite that, a Product Backlog Item has to meet the following specifications:

- o It must be a transparent unit that is deliverable.
- o Everybody in the team can see the item, discuss it, and decide how to work on it singularly or in combination with other items.
- o It must have clear criteria for successful completion.
- o It can reference other artifacts.
- o It may be completed within a single Sprint in combination with a few other Product Backlog Items. Oftentimes, items are broken down into smaller pieces to allow the team to work on them more efficiently and effectively.

It is the job of the Product Owner to maximize the value of the product over time. To do this, he or she makes sure that the most important items in the list appear towards the top.

Prioritization is quite straightforward under normal circumstances, but it can get complicated when a high-value item depends on a lower value item. So, it's important for the Product Owner to push lower value items on top of the priority list if they are part of a high-value item.

Prioritization is key in organizing the Product Backlog, but the reality is that priorities can change at any time. What was important or valuable yesterday may not be so today or tomorrow. What's more, new items arrive all the time and can be slotted in at almost any point, even towards the top of the list if the item merits it and if it is sufficiently refined.

Items in the Product Backlog are not always refined though. In fact, when a new item comes up, it's usually fuzzy and vague. Low-priority items normally don't undergo refinement, especially if they're at the bottom of the list. Top priority items, on the other hand, need to be refined and clearly defined.

The refinement process is an ongoing activity for the Product Owner and the Development Team. They work together on the item and iron out the details until they can be clearly understood by the team.

Product Backlog Refinement includes adding details and estimates. More importantly, it sets order to the items in the Product Backlog. While refining is pretty straightforward, it's the estimates that may take time to have a concession. The point of estimates is to select the amount of work for a specific Sprint. Being in a well-refined state is a consequence and a condition of their elevated status or prioritization.

What then happens to other items in the list that are not well-refined? The items at the bottom (or low-priority) are not target for refinement for the simple reason that they will not move up to the top of the list and may not be developed. The teams will not waste time refining them if the chance of them being developed is slim to none.

Understanding User Stories

User stories are written as a way of describing what the Scrum Team should build and deliver to the client. These stories are held in the Product Backlog and are used to help the team prioritize the work by value—from the highest value to the lowest.

Self-organized teams find ways to organize their work in a way that follows Agile values and principles. Before creating user stories, however, the following must be kept in mind:

- A working product or software is the primary measure of progress.
- The highest priority is to satisfy the customer through early and continuous delivery of valuable software.
- Simplicity is essential.

User stories must tell compelling stories about the value to your customers. For instance, on the product or software you are building, the story should focus on the **Who, What, and Why**. Don't include the *How*.

When writing a good user story, put yourself in the mind of the customer and think of the value that they could derive from the product. The value is what they expect when they use the product. For example, a customer wants a system that's fully functional and stable. These two requirements are what the customer will get out of the product.

Knowing your users or customers can give insights into what they want in a product. To do this, you must create rich personas that are good representations of customers. This will help the team understand the different types of customers, their priorities, and their situations.

Sometimes a user story would have multiple benefits for multiple customers. For example, an e-commerce site can benefit a customer by finding products to buy through the search functionality of the site. Another user can benefit by finding retailers in the hope of doing business with them in the future.

Writing user stories from the perspective of the user can help build the necessary parts to create value for the user. In turn, this likely means you will have to start building some of the database, but only the pieces needed to allow for the completion of each user story. When user stories are clear, the development team can focus on providing real business value to customers.

Building the application the way the user thinks about value minimizes the risk of delivering a product with the wrong features and functionalities. As user stories become much clearer, a rework may be necessary, but if you think about it, its cost is marginal compared to the perks it brings in delivering business value in the shortest possible time.

2. Sprint Backlog

This is where all the activities the Scrum Team needs to do is held. The team pulls information from the Product Backlog into the Sprint Backlog. It holds all the work for the specific Sprint goal. This is managed by the Development Team.

What can you expect in a Sprint Backlog?

- The selected Product Backlog Items for the Sprint, which the Dev Team owns in collaboration with the Product Owner.
- A list of tasks based on the Sprint goal. These tasks aim to deliver the Product Backlog.
- At least one high-priority process improvement. This was added in the Scrum guide to ensure that the team can make improvements and enhancements.

Items brought into the Sprint Backlog are forecast to be delivered, so it does not necessarily mean that the team must commit to delivering them. It would still depend on many other factors. This is where the flexibility factor of the Scrum framework comes in. Things can change during the Sprint so the Product Owner can make a decision to push through with that item or not.

3. Product Increment

Increments are working additions to the product. Every product in the Sprint must be a fully working piece of product that is potentially releasable. The increment can be made up of many releases. There's no limit to how many releases can be made in a day. The team can release as many as necessary throughout the Sprint as long they make sense and are allowed and approved by the Product Owner.

Increment is essentially the sum of all the product backlog items in a particular Sprint. It must meet the following specifications:

- o The increment must be usable and fully functional.

- o It must be potentially releasable. It doesn't have to be released when it is done; it can be made up of several releases throughout the Sprint time frame.

- o It can be made up of items delivered throughout the Sprint.

- o It must be done. This is based on the team's definition of "done". There must be a clear definition of what it's going to take for the increment to be complete. Typically, if all of the criteria are met, the increment can be considered complete and done.

Key Takeaways

- Scrum artifacts replace the formal and rigid documentation that traditional methods use.

- Scrum artifacts are dynamic, changeable, and easy to share and manage.

The next chapter discusses the main event that make Scrum happen. This covers the planning stages, the implementation, the actual Sprint, the Daily Scrum, the review, and the retrospective.

Chapter 6 Scrum Events

"Rituals bring people together, allowing them to focus on what is important and to acknowledge significant events or accomplishments." — **Luis Gonçalves**

Officially, there are five Scrum Events specified in the Scrum Guide, but it's necessary to include Scrum Grooming as a prerequisite to Sprint Planning. Each event has a specific purpose for the Scrum Team.

1. Scrum Grooming (Product Backlog Refinement)

This is the process of refining, estimating, and ordering items within the Product Backlog. Although this is not an official event in the Scrum Guide, the development team may spend 10% of their capacity supporting backlog refinement. It's just good practice for items to undergo backlog refinement before introducing them at Sprint Planning.

Holding a backlog refinement event a few days in advance of Sprint Planning can help the team discover issues and problems, and they'll have enough time to do more research before the Sprint.

The Product Owner can show the team a proposed list of Product Backlog items for refinement hours before the Scrum Grooming event. This way, the team can have a look at user stories and anticipate issues.

During this event, the whole team gathers together and starts discussing the highest-ranked backlog item. It will help tremendously if the items are on index cards or sticky notes posted on walls or whiteboards. Keep the discussion going until items meet the Definition of Ready.

When all items have been refined, the Product Owner or the Scrum Master can conclude the event and move on to Sprint Planning.

2. Sprint Planning

This is where the team looks at the Product Backlog and creates a forecast of what can be done within the Sprint time frame specified by the team. This is a critical point in the process because it sets the Sprint Goal and ensures that everything that the team does ties back to the goal.

The entire Scrum team attends this Sprint Planning so that team members will have a clear idea of what it is they are going to deliver. This is also the time to ask the Product Owner about the criteria, requirements, and specifications of the product. It's an opportunity for the members to come together to make a forecast without being too ambitious or ambiguous.

The Sprint Goal is an objective that must be met during the Sprint. It helps keep everyone focused throughout the implementation of the backlog items. With this kind of setup, the team is given enough flexibility in delivering the Increment.

It's important to remember that the Sprint Goal is fixed throughout the Sprint, but the framework allows members a little more wiggle room for the implementation of the Product Backlog Items. The team is not going to say that they will deliver exactly the set of features as presented in the Product Backlog Items because these are just forecast. What the team will do is to ensure that whatever features they are able to create and implement must be tied back to the Sprint Goal.

3. Sprint

The Sprint is essentially a container for all the activities and events of the Scrum. A Sprint duration runs for 30 days or less. It starts with Sprint Planning and ends with the Sprint Retrospective. It cannot last for more than 30 days because anything beyond that time frame and the team members start to lose focus. Then, feature creep starts to rear its ugly head.

The idea here is that you don't have to deliver the whole product in 30 days. You only need to deliver some value within that time frame. If the team can't deliver some value in that 30-day window, it's time to rethink what the team is trying to deliver. It also doesn't mean that you have to use all 30 days to deliver value. There are teams that do one-week Sprints or two-week Sprints and they are able to deliver increments without any problems.

- Sprint is the container of all Scrum events, activities, and everything in between.
- The Scrum Team focuses on developing activities to deliver value within the specified time frame.
- A Sprint starts with Sprint Planning and culminates with Sprint Retrospective.
- A Sprint must be done in 30 days or less to enable regular feedback and prevent feature creep or excessive addition of features.

Sprint Burndown Chart

The Sprint Burndown Chart is the visualization of the team's progress within the Sprint. It is a way for the Product Owner and the Scrum Team

Scrum Mastery

to monitor how the Sprint is going—and to check whether the team can accomplish the Sprint goal on time.

The graphical representation of the outstanding work vis-a-vis time is useful in predicting when the Sprint can be completed. A burndown chart is a must-have tool for the following reasons:

- Monitoring the project scope creep
- Keeping the Scrum Team on schedule
- Comparing the team's planned work against the actual work

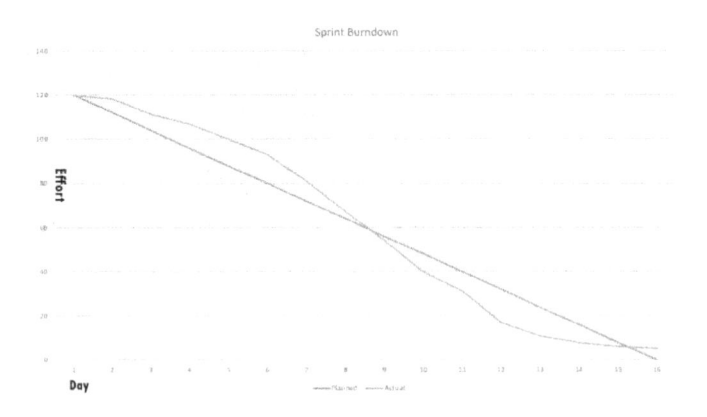

Figure 1. An Example of a Sprint Burndown Chart Comparing Planned Work vs. Actual Work

The burndown chart is also a gauge of how well (or how badly) the team is making estimates or anticipating unforeseen impediments. It can help the Product Owner and the Scrum Master figure out what's causing the team to slow down, making sure all impediments are removed to keep the team working at full speed.

4. Daily Scrum

This is a 15-minute daily meeting wherein the team looks and inspects its daily progress. Doing so allows the team to make changes and updates to the daily plan. Daily Scrum is not a status meeting. It is an opportunity for the Development Team to inspect the progress and adapt towards achieving the Sprint Goal.

It finds answers to the following questions:

- Is the team moving towards the Sprint Goal?
- Does the team need to re-plan?

- What are the things the team needs to work on to achieve the goal?
- Does the team need help?
- What critical issues need to be addressed immediately?
- What impediments have team members identified?

If there is a need to re-plan, the team can create a plan for the next 24 hours. Holding short meetings daily optimizes not just team collaboration but team performance as well.

It's also worth mentioning that team members shouldn't wait for the Daily Scrum to bring up issues and problems. The point is to report issues as they happen and not let them go unaddressed or unreported.

A Daily Scrum is necessary to share commitments, identify impediments, stay focused, increase collaboration, and maintain situational awareness.

5. Sprint Review

This is the event where the team reviews the product or increment with the stakeholders and updates the Product Backlog as necessary. Here, stakeholders can be external customers, end users, the marketing or sales department, or any group that has a stake in the project.

Stakeholders are provided a demo of the product and they are encouraged to provide feedback, criticisms, comments, reactions, or opinions for the sake of improvement. Based on the insights of the stakeholders, the Product Backlog is updated to incorporate all valuable and sensible feedback.

Sprint Review is a two-way communication process that takes into account the stakeholders' inputs. The Scrum Team, in turn, adapts by making changes in the Sprint Planning for the next Sprint.

Getting feedback is critical because it is a way to build products and features that customers actually want. What the team wants doesn't always match what the customer wants. If a team insists on delivering a product based on what the team wants, they are not delivering value to the customers. So, feedback is necessary and must be sought from stakeholders.

Sprint Review is not about selling a product. It is about communication between the team and the customers to ensure that the product being created is providing value to the end users.

Definition of Done

In the Scrum framework, Definition of Done (DoD) defines when a product or software feature is considered complete. If it meets the required quality standard set by DoD, then the product is done. This includes all the expected outcomes in design, coding, testing, validations, documentation, and non-functional requirements.

DoDs are categorized by user stories and tasks. While the DoDs of user stories focus on functional and non-functional requirements as set out in the product backlog, DoDs of tasks focus on activities from the Scrum Team members.

The Scrum Product Owner and the Scrum Team jointly define the user stories and the tasks incrementally throughout the development process—and rightfully so.

The operative word here is *incrementally*. This means that the development process allows the team to adjust their actions when the need arises. They do so in a controlled manner so that there is no added risk or costs to the project. It also prevents jeopardizing previous work or delaying the project unnecessarily.

Because the Scrum Team builds a shippable product increment at the end of each Sprint, they can discuss these with the Scum Product Owner and the stakeholders and get feedback that can be incorporated to the next steps of the project. A working product is created and if there are functionalities that need to be added, removed, or enhanced, the team will address them on the next steps.

This kind of flexibility eases not just the software development process but the operational processes as well. It optimizes the use of all the available resources and minimizes waste.

Release Planning

Release planning takes place either as part of the Sprint Review or during preparation for the subsequent Sprint.

The main goal of the Scrum Team is to provide value to customers as quickly and as efficiently as possible while keeping the development work aligned with the needs of the business. To ensure this happens, Release Planning is done. It's an opportunity for the company's vision and product roadmap to be in the same space as the people who are designated to implement it.

This sub-event helps the Development Team plan how they will execute the activities in the roadmap. It helps the team successfully work toward delivering value

There may be some confusion on the term *release*. It could mean the release of the completed product to the customer. In Scrum context, release refers to a Timebox that the team is planning for a certain time period. It specifies the goals and deliverables that the team must achieve.

The team might deliver at the end of the Timebox or spread out throughout the timeline. Essentially, release planning refers to different release cadence:

- Release after multiple Sprints
- Release every Sprint
- Release every feature

Release Planning is an opportunity for the team to make a commitment to the completion of the highest-ranked product backlog item for the upcoming Timebox. It also gives the team a chance to synchronize objectives and understand their work better.

To get started with the Release Planning meeting, you need to begin with the highest-ranked product backlog. This is the responsibility of the Product Owner in advance of the meeting. He or she works with the stakeholders and the Development Team to write user stories and rank the items in the backlog that can be successfully delivered. You also need a vision and roadmap that reflect the market and the objectives of the organizations.

A successful Release Planning meeting must align with the plans as specified with the roadmap. The meeting kicks off with the team's vision and roadmap so everyone is on the same page about the overall goal of the product.

The team then reviews the architecture and important technical information in order to understand the technology baseline for the release. A release name and theme are determined to help the team coalesce around a goal while providing focus for reviewing the user stories.

A review of the team's velocity is conduc... well as a review of the iteration schedule for this release. This lets members understand how much work will be in the release and how to best distribute it across its iterations.

It's also important for the team to review the items in their backlog against the DoD to know how much time and resources the team can commit to completing the work. The estimates need to be based on a shared definition of what it means to be done.

The point of the release planning meeting is for the Product Owner to present the highest-ranked user stories in the backlog, which should be the Scrum Team's focus in the next release.

The team reviews user stories and provides estimates typically in the form of story points. Any story that is too big to be completed in a single iteration needs to be broken down into smaller user stories so that it can be distributed appropriately during this process.

The acceptance criteria must be validated by the team so that everyone is clear on the work that needs to be done for the distribution of stories across all the iterations. If release has been completed, the team should look back and identify any issues concerning dependencies and assumptions that have come up during the meeting.

A release planning done well accomplishes more than just the plan itself. The team develops a clear understanding of the work so that they could build the most valuable product increment. The two-day planning session is a time investment worth taking to get the team on a regular release cadence and makes Sprint Planning a little less chaotic.

6. Sprint Retrospective

A Sprint Retrospective is one of the five mandatory events of Scrum. Like all other events, it is an opportunity to empirically manage some aspects of Scrum. Empiricism refers to transparency, inspection, and adaptation. This is where the team members come together and talk about what happened and discuss what worked and what didn't. It evaluates the previous Sprint and makes necessary adjustments and improvements for the next Sprint.

The intent of a Sprint Retrospective process is to encourage the Scrum Team members to pause and reflect on their interactions with one another and with the stakeholders. They inspect how effective these interactions are and then identify specific actionable improvements that they are going to make as a way of adapting their interactions in the next Sprint.

Sprint Retrospective is done after every Sprint Review. Only members of the Scrum Team should participate in this meeting. No external stakeholders are invited. This is because it is supposed to be a safe place for the team to discuss both the successes and the failures of the Sprint.

This is about inspecting how the Scrum Team works as a team and how it adapts to changes. Based on the discussion, the team identifies actionable improvements for the next Sprint.

These are hard conversations and discussions that make some people uncomfortable and vulnerable (because who wants to talk about their weaknesses, right?). This is where the Scrum Values come in. The commitment, openness, and respect among members are in full display.

The retrospective should take place after the Sprint Review for the current Sprint and then before Sprint Planning for the next Sprint. The duration is set at a maximum of three hours for a 30-day Sprint and then proportionately shorter for smaller sprints.

The Scrum Master participates as a peer and facilitates the meeting to ensure that the discussion does not go off-track.

Format

The flow of the retrospective starts with the Scrum Team discussing how the previous Sprint went—identifying things that went really well and ranking them. One of the most important agenda items for this event is to ask whether the team learned something that might help improve the quality of future increments.

Some of the things that could have gone better, especially when it comes to delivering high-quality valuable shippable increments to stakeholders, are also discussed. It's a means of identifying what the team might try to do differently in the next Sprint. To do this, the team can evaluate performance based on the DoD.

Then, the team can start looking at the interactions from different lenses. For instance, one lens could be about relationships and interactions with each other. Another lens could be tools or development practices and processes.

After talking about this, they can shift to adaptation. This is where the Scrum team organizes and identifies at least one actionable improvement that they are going to take in the next Sprint as a result of the retrospective. This step is necessary because if thoughts and ideas are not converted into adaptation or action, the retrospective may be useless. So, transparency and inspection are important for empirical management.

Participants must use this opportunity at least once every Sprint to talk about improvements so they can be implemented at any day at any time during the Sprint.

Key Takeaways

- Scrum Events cover the planning stage, implementation, review, and retrospection.
- Each event has a specific purpose and it moves the workflow along in a rapid and consistent manner.
- The events give the team the opportunity to inspect, adapt, and correct, and learn.

The next chapter shows a typical Scrum scenario to illustrate how a team uses the Scrum framework to create a product. It also lists down some real-world examples of companies that embraced Scrum and succeeded.

Chapter 7 Scrum in Action

"Thriving in today's marketplace frequently depends on making a transformation to become more agile." —Scott M. Graffius

Typical Scrum Scenario

To better understand the 3-3-5 Scrum framework, here's a project scenario that will give you an idea how Scrum works in the real world.

Traditional Method:

The goal of the company is to create a web-based trading platform. Six months prior to adopting the Scrum framework, the company had the lofty goal of completing the project and delivering all the big features of the trading platform in six months.

During those six months, the team struggled with the project because there was a lot of going back and forth on what features to change and what needs to be added or removed. The team was hell-bent on delivering the complete product based on the requirements and specifications without a proper feedback mechanism.

As a result, they ran into different kinds of problems and they attempt to fix things on the fly. Ultimately, they completed the web platform but they soon realized that they delivered the wrong product. The platform was functional but it didn't have the right features and benefits.

With Scrum Framework:

Sprint 1 – Day 0

In the Sprint Planning meeting, the Scrum Product Owner presents the stakeholder requirements and the backlog items to the Scrum team. The items should be arranged from highest to lowest priority.

The team tackles the matter of whether they have the required skills, technical know-how,

Scrum Mastery

and enough capacity and resources to complete the project. They then commit to complete user actions or user stories 1, 2, 5, 6, 8, and 9. They decided that items 3 4, and 7 cannot be realized in Sprint 1 because some resources and technical infrastructure are not yet set in place.

After the meeting, the Scrum Master rounds up the team to get their inputs on how the items, particularly those they have committed to do, are going to be carried out. Based on the details, the tasks are listed down and placed on the Sprint task board so that the team can see it. Every member of the Scrum Team picks a task which they will handle.

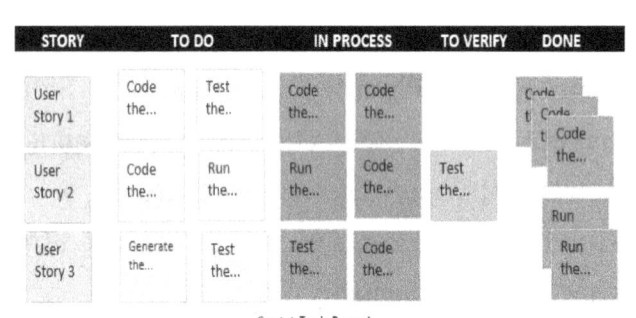

STORY	TO DO		IN PROCESS		TO VERIFY	DONE
User Story 1	Code the...	Test the..	Code the...	Code the...		Code the...
User Story 2	Code the...	Run the...	Run the...	Code the...	Test the...	Run the...
User Story 3	Generate the...	Test the...	Test the...	Code the...		Run the...

Sprint Task Board

110

Figure 2. An Example of a Generic Sprint Task Board

Sprint 1 – Day 1

The team holds their Daily Scrum Meeting in the morning to give updates on what have been done so far. The team also updates the remaining hours. Members of the team share any impediments to completing their tasks. As it turns out, one team member needs a license for the software he is using. He could not proceed without it.

The Scrum Master asks if there are other problems hindering the progress of the projects and says he'll handle them. In 15 minutes, the meeting is over. The Scrum Master orders the required licenses for the team members that need them.

Sprint 1 – Day 2

The team assembles in the morning for the Daily Scrum meeting. One team member opens up to the Scrum Product Owner about having trouble understanding a process in one of the user actions. The Product Owner explains to him the details and then he figures what he had to do to implement the action.

Sprint 1 – Day 28

On the last day, the Scrum Master invites the entire team for the Sprint Review Meeting. In 30 days, the team has managed to build a working trading platform that users can start to use.

The Product Owner evaluates the product to see if the implementation meets expectations, and if documenting the features has been properly done.

At the end of the Review Session, the Product Owner concludes:

- User stories 1, 2, 5, and 6 are completed as expected.

- User story 8 could not be completed; therefore, it was not included in the implementation.
- Story 9 needs more tweaking before it can be implemented.

In the afternoon, the team gathers for the Sprint Retrospective Meeting. They discussed the things that went well as well as those that didn't. They identified the things that can be improved.

The consensus was that there was some confusion about the overall platform architecture. The Scrum Product Owner then invites the person who designed the platform to explain the details so that everyone is on the same page.

Sprint 2 – Day 1

The Product Owner adds items to the Product Backlog based on customer feedback. He also added items that will address the shortcomings of User story 9. Taking into consideration the findings from the Retrospective Meeting, the team commits to the new user stories. With the Scrum Master serving as key facilitator, the team begins the second Sprint.

This is, of course, the simplified version of the workings of Scrum. It is quite systematic but it's by no means linear nor rigid. There's always room for discussion and correction.

You may have noticed from the example that the entire product was not delivered after 30 days. The Product Owner decided that only four of the six user actions can be implemented and delivered. Even then, the team was able to deliver a working trading platform with enough features to make the site functional. Other aspects of the site (Increments) will be implemented in the next Sprints.

The triangle of project management consists of three project success elements of time, budget, and quality. With Scrum, quality is not optional, it is mandatory. The Scrum Team works with clients in mind and strives to deliver the best possible product that can be built jointly.

Greg Caldwell

Scrum in the Real World

The combination of Agile and Scrum has gained popularity among big software development companies as well as governments and banks. Here's how they achieved tremendous success by adopting Scrum in their large-scale projects:

Adobe

- o To compete with Apple's Final Cut Pro, Adobe adopted an Agile mindset in 2008 for its Adobe Premiere Pro video editor. The first release using Scrum was Premiere Pro CS5, which delivered a substantial improvement in product quality and overall market perception.

Amazon

- o The online retail giant has been using Agile practices since 1999. Scrum became widely used across business units since 2004.
- o Scrum implementation in Amazon starts at the ground level. The system is decentralized

Scrum Mastery

and designed to let development teams deliver high-quality software.

o Amazon eliminated the silo approach so that developers can deploy codes to any of the servers. This enables them to innovate and deploy faster with little to no impediments or restrictions.

Google

o Gmail was developed using the Scrum framework.

o Multiple Scrum Teams work in synchronized Sprints on various tasks—compose functionality, spellcheck functionality, and search functionality.

o The Gmail integration team then integrates everything into the Email module.

Spotify

o How does a European startup company with a current valuation of $4 billion compete with and outperform Google, Apple, and

Amazon in the digital music service space? Spotify adopted an Agile approach to running its business.

- o Spotify recruited leading Agile trainers to take on the Scrum Master roles.
- o The company organizes teams from all over the world into clusters known as squads. Each squad is treated as an individual startup. Squads are each given a piece of a product that is completely theirs. So, they are able to change, upgrade, and deploy constantly without affecting other products.

IBM

- o The tech giant has adopted Agile Scrum in its business operations by focusing on three areas of change (People, Process, Tools). As a result, IBM experienced improvement in their metrics.
- o IBM created its proprietary management software called IBM Rational Team Concert which has Agile development integration.

Australia and New Zealand Bank (ANZ)

- In 2018, Australia's third-largest bank adopted an Agile approach using Sprint. The large-scale transition to Agile resulted in new leadership and greater efficiency. The bank handles the same level of workload with 30% less employees.

FBI Sentinel Project

- In 2006, the FBI green-lit the Sentinel project aimed at digitizing case records and automating related processes. The budget was $451 million. It was expected to be deployed to 30,000 FBI agents and personnel by December 2009.

- By August 2010, the FBI had spent $405 million but only managed to deliver functionality for two of four phases using the Waterfall method. It was a failure.

- In 2010, the project was restarted using Scrum framework.

- By 2011, the Sentinel Project was completed for $30 million.

Key Takeaways

- A typical Scrum scenario can work in a 3-3-5 Scrum framework.
- Big companies use Scrum and Agile framework to complete large-scale projects with a high level of success.

Conclusion

Traditional models of software development focus on work efficiency over value. Although they may have worked wonders for decades, the cracks in the obsolete processes have been exposed. With rigid methods and a bureaucratic approach to development, projects go over budget and over schedule. Worst of all, the products may be outdated by the time they are released to the customer.

When such an unfortunate thing happens, the product is considered a failure. Even if the product looks great or has some promising features, all that won't matter if the final product doesn't provide value to the customers and the stakeholders.

A solution to all these project management woes is Scrum. Not only does Scrum reveal the shortcomings of traditional software development practices, but it also shows the potential of the framework to accelerate the productivity of the team as well as improve the quality of products to meet or exceed customer expectations.

Scrum's unique approach to project management allows the people involved in the project to correct errors as soon as they turn up and not after the product is released to the end users.

With the Agile framework as its cornerstone, Scrum allows a flexible workflow that focuses on creating a product that provides value at every iteration. This means that every time a version of the product is released, there is a substantial benefit for the end users.

Without a leader that tends to monopolize decision-making, the team is given free rein to choose the best possible solution to deliver the best product. Guided by the Product Owner and the Scrum Master, the team is able to make the right decisions because the system allows them to.

A self-organizing Development Team does the work during Sprint which can run from a week to four weeks. During the 15-minute Daily

Scrum, the progress is monitored and inspected. This is an opportunity to find out what's working and what's not, and the team will act accordingly. This enables the Development Team to work together to deliver value once a day, ultimately making it much easier to finish the product.

Through the Sprint Review, the team is given the opportunity to interact with the stakeholders where they inspect the Sprint results together. This is followed by the Sprint Retrospective where they assess their work and suggest plans for improvement.

Organizations that use the Scrum framework in their project management and work processes derive a tremendous amount of benefits, whether tangible or intangible.

Better Product Quality

Scrum employs inspection and testing. When a Sprint is initiated, the team works on a particular product backlog item and the testing happens right there and then. This ensures that whatever work item is being created, it passes the quality based on the requirements.

Increased Time to Market

When it comes to creating a product, every company wants to be the first to release a new feature or a new iteration of the product in the market. It makes perfect sense to do so when there are many competitors in the market. With Scrum, a product (or a version of it) can be released into the market before another company does. Because of the many feedback mechanisms in place, the product becomes shippable at the quickest time possible.

Increased Return on Investment

As a result of the fast delivery of a high-quality product in the market, sales follow just as quickly. Because work is done with less time, effort, and cost, the return on investment is higher. The efficiency of Scrum enables the team to minimize errors and at the same time, reduces the risk of delivering the wrong product to the end users.

Higher Customer Satisfaction

Scrum allows the Development Team and the stakeholders to come together during the Sprint Review. This enables a steady stream of feedback about the product. The stakeholders' involvement in the process allows the team to deliver a product that fulfills the requirements. If there are features in the product that don't add value or do not match the requirements, the team can adapt and make the necessary changes. The team works with customer requirements in mind.

Higher Team Morale

With Scrum, teams are self-organized and efficient. There is a sense of ownership and responsibility. Members are committed to the project and they generally have a sense of appreciation and respect towards one another.

Their involvement in the decision-making and design process gives them a sense of pride in their work. It boosts their morale and it benefits the organization tremendously.

Increased Interaction with Stakeholders

The Sprint Review enables the Development Team to have direct access to the stakeholders—clients, customers, end users, or internal customers. The increased interaction creates a harmonious relationship that fosters transparency and openness. The more comfortable they become, the easier it is to discuss problems and find solutions.

Increased Collaboration and Ownership

The work processes under the Scrum framework encourage collaboration and engagement. This creates an environment that is conducive for people to thrive and excel in their work. It also encourages transparency so the entire team knows what's going on. There are no surprises or inexplicable events that could derail the progress of the team.

Reduced Risk

Because there is constant inspecting and adapting during Sprints, the team is able to do some mid-course corrections to fix errors. It prevents finding critical issues very late in the development of the product. This kind of monitoring reduces the risk of delivering a product with the wrong features or poor functionalities. The risk of failing is greatly reduced because every step is taken to avoid disappointing the customers and the end users.

All in all, Scrum provides an empirical foundation that enables teams to deliver products or iterations more frequently with higher value and better outcomes to customers. If you want to transform your organization to create higher-value products and make customers happy, you must adopt the Scum framework into the work processes of your

Greg Caldwell

project management or software development teams.

Scrum Mastery

Thank you

Before you go, I just wanted to say thank you for purchasing my book.

You could have picked from dozens of other books on the same topic but you took a chance and chose this one.

So, a HUGE thanks to you for getting this book and for reading all the way to the end.

Now I wanted to ask you for a small favor. **Could you please consider posting a review on the platform? Reviews are one of the easiest ways to support the work of independent authors.**

This feedback will help me continue to write the type of books that will help you get the results you want. So if you enjoyed it, please let me know!

Click here to leave a review!

https://www.amazon.com/review/create-review/

Resources Page

Association for Project Management. (n.d.). Agile Methods. Retrieved November 11, 2019, from https://www.apm.org.uk/resources/find-a-resource/agile-project-management/agile-methods/

Green, P. (2012). Adobe Premiere Scrum Adoption. Retrieved November 12, 2019, from http://blogs.adobe.com/agile/files/2012/08/Adobe-Premiere-Pro-Scrum-Adoption-How-an-agile-approach-enabled-success-in-a-hyper-competitive-landscape-.pdf

O'Connor, G. (2016). Agile must-haves: three requirements for a great agile team. PM Network, 30(1), 26–27.

Schwaber, K., & Sutherland, J. (2017, November). The Scrum Guide: Retrieved November 9, 2019, from https://www.scrumguides.org/docs/scrumguide/v2017/2017-Scrum-Guide-US.pdf#zoom=100

Sims, C., & Johnson, H. L. (2012). The Elements of Scrum [Epub]. United States: Dymaxicon.

Sims, C., & Johnson, H. L. (2014). Scrum: A Breathtakingly Brief and Agile Introduction [Epub]. United States: Dymaxicon.

Sliger, M. (2011). Agile Project Management with Scrum. Paper presented at PMI Global Congress 2011—North America, Dallas, TX. Newtown Square, PA: Project Management Institute.

Sutherland, J., & Sutherland, J. J. (2014). *Scrum: The Art of Doing Twice the Work in Half the Time* [Epub]. New York: Currency.

International Scrum Institute. (2019). The Scrum Framework. Retrieved from https://www.scrum-institute.org/contents/The_Scrum_Framework_by_International_Scrum_Institute.pdf

Sutherland, J. (2014, January 23). Scrum Done Right: How Spotify Takes On Industry Giants | OpenView Labs [Blog post]. Retrieved November 17, 2019, from https://openviewpartners.com/blog/spotify-great-agile-example-scrum-done-right/#.XdUvE1cza00

Takeuchi, H., & Nonaka, I. (1986). The New Development Game. Harvard Business Review, 3–10. Retrieved from https://ullizee.files.wordpress.com/2013/01/takeuchi-and-onaka-the-new-new-product-development-game.pdf